# Under the Sea

TIPS, TECHNIQUES, INSPIRATIONAL RAMBLINGS, CREATIVE NUDGINGS AND STEP-BY-STEP INSTRUCTIONS TO HELP YOU CREATE

CHRISTI FRIESEN

Welcome to book 3
of the CF Sculpture Series - Under the Sea.
I'm a water person, love it, love it, love it - from a big
ol' glass of ice water, to a refreshing float in a pool, to mucking around
under rocks in a creek to see
what creatures come out,
I'm a fan.

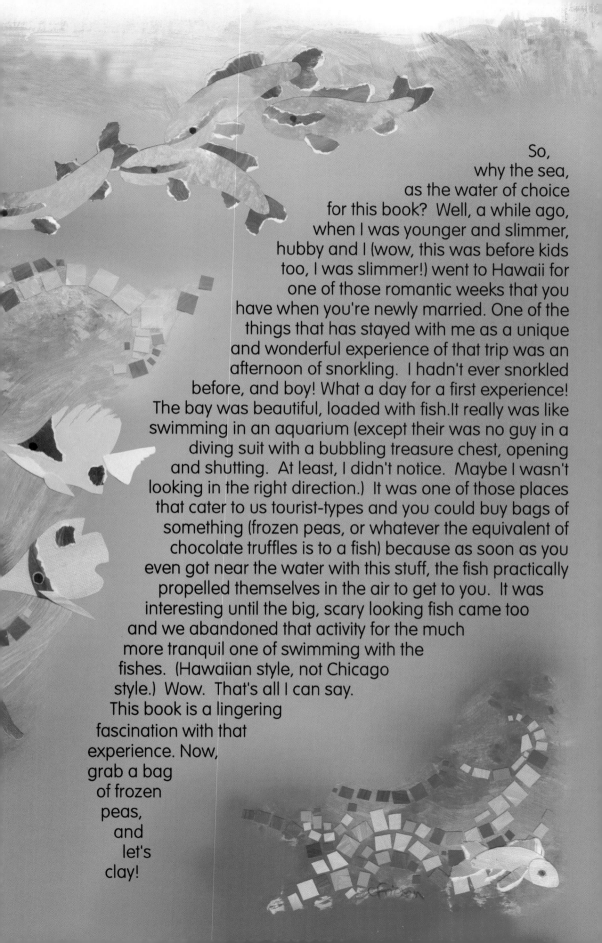

So,
why the sea,
as the water of choice
for this book?  Well, a while ago,
when I was younger and slimmer,
hubby and I (wow, this was before kids
too, I was slimmer!) went to Hawaii for
one of those romantic weeks that you
have when you're newly married. One of the
things that has stayed with me as a unique
and wonderful experience of that trip was an
afternoon of snorkling.  I hadn't ever snorkled
before, and boy! What a day for a first experience!
The bay was beautiful, loaded with fish.It really was like
swimming in an aquarium (except their was no guy in a
diving suit with a bubbling treasure chest, opening
and shutting.  At least, I didn't notice.  Maybe I wasn't
looking in the right direction.)  It was one of those places
that cater to us tourist-types and you could buy bags of
something (frozen peas, or whatever the equivalent of
chocolate truffles is to a fish) because as soon as you
even got near the water with this stuff, the fish practically
propelled themselves in the air to get to you.  It was
interesting until the big, scary looking fish came too
and we abandoned that activity for the much
more tranquil one of swimming with the
fishes.  (Hawaiian style, not Chicago
style.)  Wow.  That's all I can say.
This book is a lingering
fascination with that
experience. Now,
grab a bag
of frozen
peas,
and
let's
clay!

# TOOLS & SUPPLIES

white

pearl

ecru

gold

green pearl

sap green

turquoise

these are
some of the
colors used in
this book

ultramarine
blue

blue
pearl

copper

burnt umber

for all the projects in this book, but you'll probably just want to have these for all your clay adventures

## POLYMER CLAY

I use Premo! (a Sculpey product) because it is just right for sculpting -- not too firm, not too soft and very durable once cooked.

liquid clay - Sculpey brand Translucent Liquid Clay

pasta machine
cardstock (or index cards) to work on
oven/oven thermometer
acrylic paint (for patina.) browns are my patina color of choice, (although you can also use blues and greens)  -- I always have on hand burnt umber, burnt sienna and raw sienna.
clear coating
brushes and sponges

## tools

These are my favorite tools.

RNT 1&2  a cool tool with interchangeable ends

Ceramic tool AJ17
(this one is my favorite favorite!)

KEMPER TOOLS JA17

see the back of the book for info on where to get these items.

# More tools

needle tool
needlenose tweezers
cutting blade
wire cutters and pliers
wire -- 28 gauge craft wire of any color for all the wiring of the beaded embellishments and thicker wire (16 or 18 gauge) for hangers and for creating beading holes during sculpting
(don't worry, I'll explain what all this means)

# beads

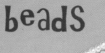

here's what I used in these projects, but you can use anything similar in glass, ceramic, metal, crystal, stone or pearl!

pearls (there are so many shapes, sizes and colors now to choose from -- just use lots -- remember, it's art, so that justifies going on a shopping spree!)

art glass beads (there are sooooo many to chose from! So many wonderful glass artists using an amazing variety of glass types and creative styles. Use whatever your favorites are. If you don't want to use art glass, any glass bead or crystal will work also.)

dichroic glass cabs

semiprecious stones (faceted, round, faceted. . . use 'em all! You can never have enough semiprecious stones! I used jade, turquoise, peridot, and lots of others.)

black onyx, garnet, lapis (or any dark, round bead) 3mm or 4mm for eyes!

shells

chocolate, preferably european and semi-sweet or dark (you can't use it in the sculptures, of course, but it just won't be as much fun creating without it!)

# Turtle time!

Every ocean needs a turtle, so let's start by making one, or two, or eight (they're addictive).

So whadda' ya say we start with mixing up some clay colors. One wad for the shell (top and bottom) and one wad for the body bits. You can make your turtle any color you want, of course, as your mood dictates. We'll do the generic but lovely, green-ish tan-ish color that is all the rage for sea turtles this fashion season. The tan-ish color is ecru, mostly, with a bit of green and gold in it, and the green-ish color is the same thing with more green in it (you can use green or green pearl, or even sap green for a similar color.)

For the top shell, roll a ball of either color (I used the tan-ish one) about the size of a large gumball (you know the kind you can hardly close your mouth around which makes you drool. ick.) The bottom shell is a smaller ball of the same color. Flatten it with your fingers until it's the thickness of a silver dollar and about the size of a quarter.

For the top shell, form it with your hands (I suppose you can use your toes, but it takes a lot of practice) into an egg shape and flatten it a bit - but only on the bottom of the egg - keep that top rounded, a nice curvy shell shape, don't ya know! Ok, so the top shell shape should be able to cover over the bottom shell, no parts showing (don't put it on top yet, just check it and tweak the clay if necessary).

Now let's make the head. Use the green-ish color and roll out a little log of clay. Don't forget that some of the neck will be under the shell, so make it longer than necessary.

Use your fingers to gently pinch the nose end to a bit of point - not too much, just a nice turtle snout kind of point.

Use your thumb and forefinger to gently pinch on either side of the head (snout side) to create a slight depression that will become the eye socket area.

If you squish it too hard and make a bulge on the forehead, just press it back down.

If you've read either of my previous books, you know that coming up is the "wiring in the beads" lecture. If you already know all about this, you can hum quietly to yourself during the next paragraph or two.

The eyes are beads, wired and pressed into the clay. I like to use round dark beads for the eyes, these are 4 mm. black onyx. I feel adding beads to your polymer clay sculptures opens a whole new world of clay fun but you have to make the beads stay in. What you're doing is taking a glass bead thing and pressing it into a plastic. Works ok when the clay is soft and grabby, but once it's cooked and hardened, those beads can have a bad habit of popping out, which is no fun. So, wire 'em in! Oh sure, you say, the wire doesn't stick to clay any better than the glass, so what's the dealio? How astute of you, you are so very right. I've found that twisting on a little wire tail and then pressing in the bead, (which gives the clay that slightly irregular shape of the wire to harden around) holds the bead in pretty securely.

Ok, that was the lecture, you hummers can pay attention again. Unless you already know the how-to part of this as well, in which case, hum one more stanza and we'll catch up with you shortly.

Here's the standard wiring technique that will work for wiring any single bead. We'll use it now for the eye and later for everything else.

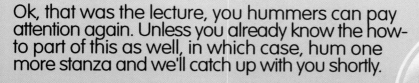

Begin by snipping a piece of 28 gauge wire - an inch or so will do it. Thread the bead onto the wire and pull the wires up so that the bead is in the middle with the wires parallel. Pinch the wires together and hold them with the pliers, about a quarter of an inch or so from the bead. Twirl the bead with your fingers to twist the wire up to the base of the bead, you will only need about an eighth of an inch or so of twist. Cut off the excess wire. Do the same with the other bead, for the other eye.

You can add the eye beads to the head right now, or we can make the little eye pancakes first -- they look really cute, so why not! Make two little balls of clay and place them in the center of the eye socket areas and flatten to make lil' pancakes ( I used some of the shell clay color for contrast.)

Add the eye beads, wire-end first, right in the center of the pancakes. I suggest that you press the beads in gently at first to make sure the placement is right. At this point your turtle will look like one of those rubber toys that you squeeze and they get all googley-eyed. Once you're satisfied with the placement of the beads, press them into the head - I like to press both in at the same time so I can use the pressure of each finger against the other, instead of smashing one side and then the other side - it works for me. If you poke through with your wire to the other side, we need to fix that - unless you want a frankenstine monster turtle. (Just pull the eye out and clip some wire off and jam it in again.) You should make sure the eye beads get pressed in about halfway - with any luck the wires will be covered. Ain't he cute! To increase the cuteness factor by 25-68%, you can add a smile. You don't have to, but why not! I like to start with a small smile and see how that works - you don't want to end up with a turtle that looks like the Joker from Batman with a maniacal grin (at least I don't think you do.) Anyway, I used the tip of my favorite wooden tool to press in to make this little grin. (If you don't have this tool go get one!! See the resources section at the end of the book.) If he needs a bit more smile, use the other end of that tool, or a needle tool to extend the corners of the mouth.

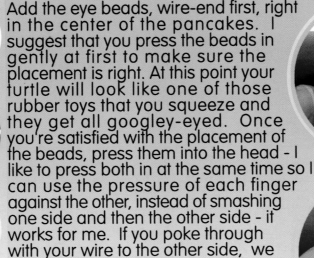

Now you can add the head to the bottom shell - all the turtle bits will be pressed on to the bottom shell, and then the top shell will cover it all. Leave most of the neck sticking out, the shell will end up covering a lot of it.

don't mind us -- we're on our way to page 36

On to the flippers. The front flippers are the powerhouse (well they would be if clay turtles could actually swim), so they will be quite a bit bigger than the back flippers. Make two balls of clay (the same color clay as the head) and roll each into a teardrop shape. Flatten it with your fingers (if you roll it thru the pasta machine it will be too flat.) Flatten the tip of the flipper more than the area that will be closest to the shell. More aerodynamically sound. Attach the flippers to the bottom shell on both sides with the points sticking out. We will play with the positioning after we're all done putting the turtle together.

some toe ideas

If you want, you can add some notches to the flippers to indicate toes, or some flattened little ovals of clay that look like toenails.

Now a little tail. Sea turtles have tails, I looked it up. Roll a little piece of the same color clay into a little snake and press that on to the bottom shell also. You can even curl the tip, so cute.

Back legs are two smaller tear-drops, flattened and attached to the shell, as well (rounded end out this time.)

Now is the time to add a wire to hold open a hole for later if your turtle is going to become a focal bead.

metal 18-14g

Shell time! Before you put the top shell on, you can press a notch into the shell for his head to peak out of.

Also, you can scallop the shell edge.

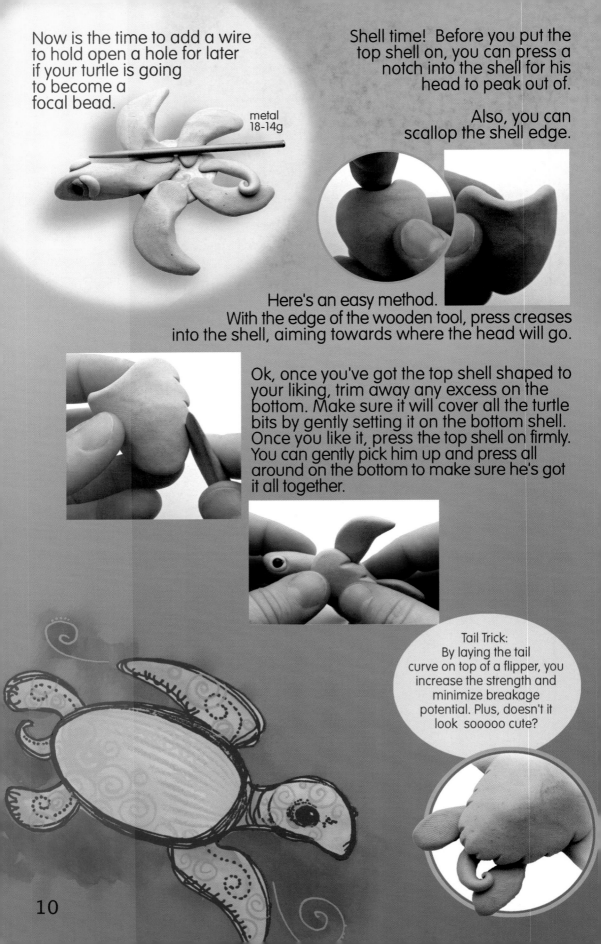

Here's an easy method. With the edge of the wooden tool, press creases into the shell, aiming towards where the head will go.

Ok, once you've got the top shell shaped to your liking, trim away any excess on the bottom. Make sure it will cover all the turtle bits by gently setting it on the bottom shell. Once you like it, press the top shell on firmly. You can gently pick him up and press all around on the bottom to make sure he's got it all together.

Tail Trick:
By laying the tail curve on top of a flipper, you increase the strength and minimize breakage potential. Plus, doesn't it look sooooo cute?

Now to make him ever so charming - it's all in the head tilt. Pull the head up and twist and turn until you go "ahhhhh". That's the look. Now prop the head up in that position so that it won't sag, tear or go droop in the oven.

use a roll of paper as a prop

And now all the hard work is done (that wasn't really hard work, was it?) and all the rest is the fun part - embellishing! Using clay and bead accents, let's turn this turtle into a cool dude. One option is to add little dots of clay to the flippers, tail, neck and face (I usually stop by the time I reach the eye area and leave his snout free of dots. It just seems better that way.)

A good way to start the shell embellishments is to pick an accent bead or pearl (here I used a lampwork glass bead), wire it in the same way as you did the eye bead, and jam it into the center of the shell. The other accent bits will come to you as you work your way around the bead. I started by covering the larger hole (and wire) that an art glass bead will always have by making a little snake of clay, curling up one end and pressing that onto the shell, using the curl to cover the hole (pretty slick, huh?) Now start adding dots and swirls of clay as you wish. I also added additional beaded goodies - pearls and olive jade. Once your turtle looks properly decked out, stop! (sometimes the embellishments can take over, hee hee.)

I am one cool dude

11

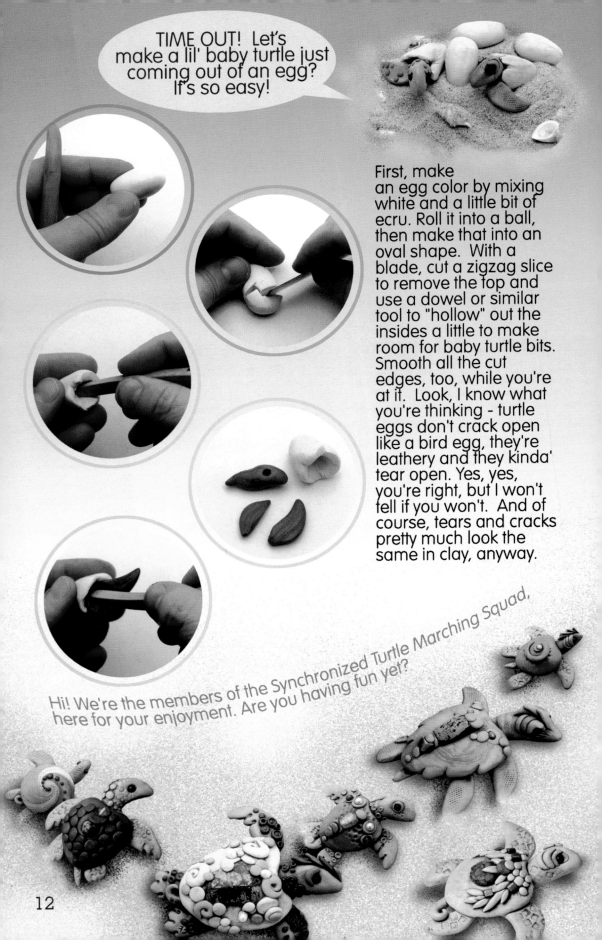

**TIME OUT!** Let's make a lil' baby turtle just coming out of an egg? It's so easy!

First, make an egg color by mixing white and a little bit of ecru. Roll it into a ball, then make that into an oval shape. With a blade, cut a zigzag slice to remove the top and use a dowel or similar tool to "hollow" out the insides a little to make room for baby turtle bits. Smooth all the cut edges, too, while you're at it. Look, I know what you're thinking - turtle eggs don't crack open like a bird egg, they're leathery and they kinda' tear open. Yes, yes, you're right, but I won't tell if you won't. And of course, tears and cracks pretty much look the same in clay, anyway.

Hi! We're the members of the Synchronized Turtle Marching Squad, here for your enjoyment. Are you having fun yet?

12

Once your shell is ready, make a little turtle head and little flippers. Stick the flipper in the hole first, then the neck and squeeze a bit to make sure everything is in. Awwwwww, sweet. Remember that turtles lay a bunch of eggs at a time, so you might want to make whole clutch of little babies.

press in the flippers with a tool to make space for the head

the grip of a needle tool makes an easy texture

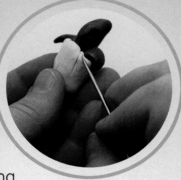

add some shell cracks

And now, back to our regularly scheduled turtling.

So, how's he looking? Fabulous? Of course.

Your turtle can be a little sculpture (put him in a dish of sand with some of the babies, and some shells and pebbles and enjoy!) or he could be a bead (if you did the wire-inside trick) to string on a necklace, OR he can be added to a little clay ocean scene and become a wall hanging which would clearly show all your friends what exquisite taste you have in decor (not to mention bragging rights when you get to casually remark that you actually made that piece.) So, on we go to making an ocean for him to live on.

This is what can happen when you just want to add a little smile and it gets out of control.

The shells on these guys feature a swirled pattern. It's a zen thing.

You can really, really scallop the edges if you want to!! (although it sorta' makes him look like a pine cone).

This one features the long lines on the shell, like a loggerhead turtle. The row of jasper beads in the middle is one wire with the ends hidden by extra bits of clay

This is another lineup of beads, carnelian this time, and going from small to big to small again, which is a nice trick to use sometimes.

This is Saint Tortuga, you can tell from the turtle halo.

13

I'm not a caner, so I won't even pretend that this is the ideal way for making canes. There are some wonderful canes in the world of polymer clay, and many books that go into it in delicious detail. But this one is kind of a cheatin' cane - it uses the idea of caning, but none of the technical skills, patience or precision of a real cane - but it's quick and easy, and provides instant gratification.

Ok, first step is to make a bunch of oceany colors  I used white, blue pearl, green pearl, and plain ol' pearl.  Make a nice selection of mixes and then run each of them through your pasta machine on the middle setting so that they are thinner.  You can chop them into roughly even rectangles if you want to, but no measuring - that will mess it all up (not really).  Now stack 'em!  Press the stack together, and run it through the pasta machine at the widest setting.

If you want really thin little lines (for a more subtle look), you can fold it in half and run it through again.  Now fold the sheet of clay back and forth, like pleats of fabric. Make some irregular lengths and then press the pleated clay together a bit to make the clay grab. Slice a thin section from your cheatin' cane and smooth/flatten with your

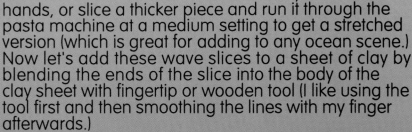

hands, or slice a thicker piece and run it through the pasta machine at a medium setting to get a stretched version (which is great for adding to any ocean scene.) Now let's add these wave slices to a sheet of clay by blending the ends of the slice into the body of the clay sheet with fingertip or wooden tool (I like using the tool first and then smoothing the lines with my finger afterwards.)

Once you've added the wave slices, time to add the turtle and any other little touches that will complete the look.  For an extra secure attachment, a little splooch of liquid clay will make sure he doesn't go anywhere after baking.

For baking details, go to page 46 or just keep reading, you'll get there eventually.

14

These are lampwork glass beads, on their sides with liquid clay underneath and up through the hole and bulging out the top a little to hold them in place.

These are just little dots of liquid clay. Adds a nice little touch, huh?

These swirls are just loose snail curls of clay. Press into place and blend the tip out into the background with your finger.

This is a wired-in art glass bead, done the same way as the one on the turtle's shell. I even hid the wire and bead hole with the same kind of swirls of clay.

The last step is to make a way to hang it on the wall. One of the nice things about adding the curls as a design element, is that you can echo them on the top as a hanger. Make the curl thicker, (and I recommend that you add another curl as a second layer on the back, for added strength.)

Ta dah! All done. Bake, patina and you're ready to hang.
(More on this at the end of the book.)

Well, that was fun. Ready to make some more? Me too. Let's make a bigger, more detailed, super-fun, fully-loaded ocean to add more sea creatures to! Come on!

Ahhhhh, colors! One of my favorite things about polymer clay is the way it lends itself to playing with colors -- stripes, blends, smears, streaks, planned color tricks and unplanned ones. Ok, sure we did some stuff already with the wave cane and that was fun and all, but wait! there's more. This section will deal with a little more advanced color magic - so let's make a bigger wall piece, one with lots of color tricks, and one that we can jam full of ocean creatures!

Let's use several colors of Premo in different combinations to make "lookat blends" to combine for a wall piece. White, pearl, blue pearl, green pearl, ecru, turquoise and ultramarine blue. I don't always precondition each color before combining them because the clays will vary slightly in consistency - some softer and some harder - which can work in your favor when blending. The softer ones spread out differently than the firmer clays and help create a richer variety of smears, stretch marks, crinkles and swooshes that make the end result more interesting. As you place several colors together and run them through the pasta machine on the widest setting, look each pass over carefully and fold the clay so that you keep the most interesting colors in front. If you need to, rip and reposition pieces to keep the cool stuff where you can see it -- don't let it get folded up inside and lost from view!

there are more details in the back about lookat blends!

Ok, got some good stuff? I suggest trying for some deeper blue mixes (more blue pearl or ultamarine blue in the blend) for the bottom of the sea; some medium blues (turquoise can be used more prominently here) for the middle of the sea; and some light colors (use much more pearl and white here) for the top and waves. Of course you will be using white and pearl in all the mixes to keep it from getting too dark.

Now piece together the blends to create the undersea adventure backdrop! Rip the clay sheets for yummy uneven lines and lay them on each. Make sure your final piece won't be any bigger than will fit in your oven! (been there, done that). It's a good idea to measure your cooking space and mark it off on a piece of paper and then work in that space. Sometimes details have a habit of meandering farther than you expect -- waves flow, seaweed wiggles, starfish scoot -- so give yourself borders to stay within.

I think it's nice to work a little wild and untamed when blending the colors - go with the flow and just let the inspiration wash over you (I could have promised you that there wouldn't be any ocean-related puns or word play, but you know that I'd just be lying.) Use your hot little hands to blend the edges where two clay sheets meet by dragging the top layer of clay over the lower layer. Vary the direction when it seems appropriate. If an area seems too rough, keep smoothing with your fingers until it's a more soft and gradual blend. Allow yourself to be free with the blending - if you try to make all the fingerprints go away and have a calm, smooth ocean, you'll be fighting a losing battle and it won't be any fun - and if it's not fun, why do it? (I say that about cooking and doing the dishes, too, by the way.)

add more blend if you need to, to get the final shape you want

As you play with the top of the piece, add some wavey ripples by tearing a piece of the lighter clay blend (doesn't the ripped edge look more frothy?) and press along that edge with thumb and forefinger to make it thinner. As it gets thinner, it will also stretch, which makes the rippley effect. You can add a couple layers for a "slightly choppy swells" look (I was going to make a pun about how "swell" that looks, but really, how many puns can you get away with before you lose all credibility?)

Now, something that adds a nice bit of stylized detail to the semi-realistic look of the blend is to add some little curls. I think it's wavey. Start by taking a bit of clay from

the extra bits you probably have from making all the background (these should have some streaks of other colors in them for the best effect). Roll a piece into a log, then twist it to make those streaks of color line up nicely. Pinch or roll into a soft point on one end and then curl that into a loose snail curl and press it on wherever you think your ocean needs it. You can blend the other end into the background, or not!

Here's another little fun thingy. Remember the stack of colors we made for the ocean wave cheat-cane? Well, if you have some of that stack left (before you folded it into pleats),cut it (about an inch wide)

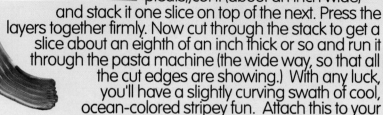

and stack it one slice on top of the next. Press the layers together firmly. Now cut through the stack to get a slice about an eighth of an inch thick or so and run it through the pasta machine (the wide way, so that all the cut edges are showing.) With any luck, you'll have a slightly curving swath of cool, ocean-colored stripey fun. Attach this to your background for some visual excitement! (I used my trusty wooden tool to blend the more boring side into the base clay.)

Here's one more cool trick to impress your friends. Use that same sheet of layered clay colors that you just used for the wave cheatin' cane and for the "stack 'em up" (or another sheet just like it if you used it all up already!) Take a piece that's about 3-4 inches long and roll it up like a scroll. Press it together firmly. Now curve it over your finger to make a bend and slice little slivers off the surface with a sharp blade tool to reveal the layers of color. Nifty! Attach this to your background by pressing.
Ok, look good so far?

A word about using pearl clay: you'd expect to use a lot of pearl clay in an ocean, wouldn't you? Alas, pearl clay does tend to brown more readily when cooked than other colors (well, translucent does too). So when using it, mix it half and half with white (which isn't so prone to scorching) and you'll keep the nice shimmery shine that pearl adds while avoiding that "polluted ocean" look of burnt clay.

17

Add any last dots, curls or bits of color and step back and give your background a good look - is everything balanced? Alrighty then, let's give this sea a proper sandy bottom.

Oooh, you're going to like this part 'cuz a new tool is involved. I've never met a polymer clayer yet that didn't love new tools!

First mix up sand color - I've used ecru with a bit of gold, a dab of copper and a smidgen of burnt umber. If you like a more sugary sand color, add some white clay, too. As you blend the clays together in the pasta machine you can leave streaks in or mix all the way to a solid color.

When the mix is complete, roll it through the pasta machine one last time to make a strip, and attach that to the bottom of the ocean blend. Hmmm, still needs something, doesn't it? Oh, if only we had a tool of some kind to make the texture in the sand!

Hee hee hee - sand-texture-making tool coming up...

Ready? Ok! Get a blob of clay (scrap clay or some hideous color mix that you'll never use will do nicely) and roll it into an oval or egg shape (I prefer an egg shape).

Now, run to the cupboard, or possibly the supermarket, and get some raw sugar (nice big grains) and some rock salt (really big grains) and some of those little round sprinkles that you use to decorate cupcakes. Put some of the rock salt on a hard surface (use a mortar and pestle if you have one, but really, who does these days?) and with something hard - spoon, hammer, teenager's head - crush the rock salt until you have some smaller but still nicely irregular salt crumbles. Dispose of any that are really big, and then put the remainder in bowl or plate. To that, add equal parts of the sugar and sprinkles. Mix 'em all together.

Throw in the ball of clay and roll it around firmly in the mix, embedding the various grains deeply into the clay. Put the weird blob on a piece of cardstock, pop it in the oven and bake! (275°F for at 30-45 minutes.) Fill a bowl with hot water and dump in the encrusted clay (while it's still hot) - the water will dissolve all the weird mix away and you will be left with a pitted ball of clay!

Once it's cooled and dried off, roll it over your strip of sand clay, and ta dah! Fabulous sand texture! (Especially when it gets some patina rubbed in.)

If the tool starts sticking to the clay, you can dust it up with cornstarch.

18

dichroic
glass beads

lapis

glass seed beads

turquiose

pearls

lamp
worked
glass beads

Since polymer clay cures at such a low baking temperature, this opens up all kinds of possibilities when it comes to adding embellishments and accents! Since anything that can be baked unharmed for an hour at 275°F can be added, this means that metals, glass, semiprecious stones, gems, pearls, ceramics and shells can all be used.

So for the next bit of sculpting, let's add some goodies! To begin, I chose a lampworked glass art bead.  Art beads are beautiful and this is a wonderful way to show them off.  Since most are much larger than a typical glass seed bead or semiprecious stone bead, we'll use a few tricks to keep them integrated into the scene - the idea is always to make it look like the bead belongs there - as if it just grew out of the clay naturally, not just dropped accidentally by a distracted bead fairy.

wired
lampwork
bead

Wire the bead the same way as you did for the turtle eye, except add a little hook at the end by bending the wire back on itself.  This will ensure a really firm grip of bead to clay - we don't want these big babies popping out and escaping!

Push the glass bead into the clay (press the bead itself in pretty firmly to embed it a bit.) It looks fun right here.  I used thick curls of clay to hide the side of the bead where the large hole is.  This adds to that smoothly integrated look.

Now how about a big turquoise bead?  Same steps, but since the hole to hide is smaller, a couple dots of clay will do the trick.  Ooh, now how about some larger round lapis beads tucked in here?  Smooth the clay as needed to keep all the lines flowing.

contact info for the
glass artists who
created the beads
for these projects is
in the back of the book

# Hey!

what?

Look what I found! Delicious dichroic cabs. Mmmm. Gotta' add those. Since they have no holes for wiring, you have to make sure that the clay accents you add will hold them in securely, but without overwhelming them by covering them up too much. Start with a gloop of liquid clay. Remember liquid clay isn't a glue, it won't bond it to the clay permanently, but it will help make the attachment firm when coupled with the clay grabbers. You can use that good ol' standby - loose snail curls, but other shapes of clay would work too.

## DON'T STOP NOW, WE'Re ON a ROLL!

these are cornflake pearls with the holes drilled underneath - mmmmmm

One more fun beaded embellishment trick is to make a lineup of beads for a dramatic curving accent. Start with a piece of wire about 2 inches long and bend a hook in the end (it keeps the wire from pulling out of the clay.) Now thread a row of beads onto the wire. Cut off any excess wire so that you end up with about an eighth of an inch or slightly more on either side of the bead row, and bend that end into a hook as well. You want enough wire to grab the clay, but not so much that it is unwieldy. Yeah, that's the right amount.

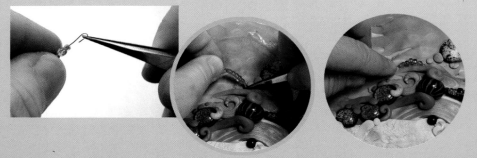

I like to use the needlenose tweezers to push the wired bead strings in - they're good for getting it right where you want it when your fingers are just too large or unwieldy (don't ya sometimes just have those unwieldy kind of days?). Cover any hole the tweezers leave behind, and any exposed wire with a little dot of clay.

Now, onwards and upwards -- time to make seaweed!

Seaweed is fun and easy to make. It provides a good contrast to the ocean colors as well as giving seahorses a lovely spot to hang out. (Seahorses are coming up - hooray!)

lookat blends

Start, as always, with some color blends. You know, seaweedy colors - I used various greens and ecru and gold. Make those fun lookat blends so that you have some nice streaks and stripes to work with. I used one color for the weeds that will be in the background and a different one for the weeds that will be on top of them - adds some depth.

I snuck in some more pearls when you weren't looking!

Cut some nice weedy shapes - I used a long, freeform leaf shape. Start with some broad ones for the background layer and lay that down first, pressing them into the background clay.

top leaves

Now the top weeds. Also freeform shape, but thinner. To soften the cut edges of each leaf shape, pick each leaf up and squeeze all along the edges. A soft squeeze will make a nice finished look, a hard squeeze will ripple the edges and make a convincing "swaying in the currents" kind of look.

Add the top layer of weeds - use lots of twists and wiggles - over the background weeds. I find that just one good press here and there as you are laying the leaves down will connect them, and also keep their fullness.

tendrils beginning

and twisting

You can add little tendrils too by slicing thin strips and twisting them (pinch the tip into a point for a more realistic look.)

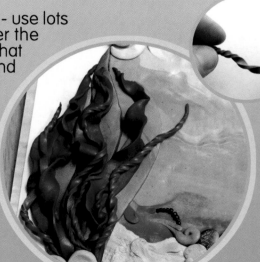

and added to the seaweed patch

21

Are you ready to add something more to the ocean bottom, near all those groovy seaweed fronds? How about some sea anemones and starfish!

I'm using a borosilicate glass bead for the sea anemones" bodies - you can use any round glass bead, or make it out of clay instead. The glass beads just look more awesome, dude.

In order to make the glass bead stick to the sandy bottom and also have a way to easily attach those wavy arm things that sea anemones have, let's roll out a little snake of clay and thread it through the hole of the bead. Roll the clay up on both sides of the bead and flatten a little so that you have a knob of clay sticking up out of top and bottom.

Put a little gloop of liquid clay on the sandy bottom where you want to attach the anemone. (It helps lock it in really good.) Press the clay knob into the liquid clay. With a dowel tool, or something similar, ream out the hole so that the clay inside the bead is packed tightly and pushed aside to leave a hole for the arms to fit in.

Put a little dot of liquid clay in the hole and now start sticking in the arms. What, you didn't make any arms? Oh, I didn't tell you to? Ok. Sorry. Arms are easy, just make little rice-shaped pieces of clay. (For a little interest, I took two colors of clay, made little logs and twisted them together and folded in half, then twisted and folded in half again, then twisted until it was a nice subtle stripey mix. Now make the little rice bits from that clay, if you wanna'.)

Pack in as many arms as will fit. Now tweak 'em! Spread them down and around, imagining a nice current making them do that slow motion dance they do.

I had more borosilicate beads, so I made some more anemones.

Ok, now we're going to add some other things because I have these really neat beads that will look great. I couldn't tell you what sort of coral reef creature they are supposed to be exactly, but they look fun and the anemone beads said that they approved, so it's ok. These are flat, disc-shaped glass beads with a little riffle around the edges. Now use a round bead (this one is olive jade about 3-4mm) and thread it onto a length of wire (about 4 inches or so), fold up the wire, and twist as if for a single bead, then thread it through one or two of the riffley beads. Trim off any excess and fold the end of the wire back, to make that handy hook. Add a gloop of that liquid clay again and stick that bead stack in! (Needlenose tweezers make this a breeze.)

Now make more of them all over! I also did the same trick with this delicious knobby lampwork glass bead too - all together they look like quite a nice little nautical community, don't they?

This is a long strand of peridot chips. Anchor the middle of the strand in one or two places with a little bent staple of wire to hold it steady.

To add a string of lampwork glass beads, use the same wiring method as for a strand of glass seed beads -- just have more wire sticking out from each end to really grab the clay. Use the fold-over hooks in the wire, too, and hide the ends with some clay accents.

23

# now let's add starfish!

Start with a ball of clay and flatten it a little. We'll be pinching out the arms one at a time. Start by pinching the first one, and pinch all around to make a point - like sharpening a pencil. (It should look like a birdie head.) Now pull and pinch the second arm (hello, kitty). Now arm three (duck's foot), and arm four (Lisa Simpson's head). Finally arm five, which will take a little finessing to pull out, but you can do it. Remember all the arms should be about the same size (I've made these short and stocky, but you can make them longer if you want.) I like to finish the look of the star by holding it on my pinkie (or anything pinkie sized and shaped) to pillow up the center. Finally, tweak the arms to make them lifelike (of course, with a starfish, how would you know?) Bend 'em, twist 'em.

For your starfish to really look his grooviest, add clay and bead accents. Start with a little dot of clay in the center. Wire up a single bead (I suggest a round one) and squoosh it right on down through that clay dot. Now add more balls of clay, in that same contrasting color, all the way down the arms. I like to add a seed bead to some of those clay dots by pressing it into the clay so that the circle part shows. I don't wire these in, as that would interfere with the look of the accent. In order to help make sure those beads stay put, I add a thin smear of liquid clay over the top of the bead and into the hole. Lastly, you can add texture with a pointy tool.

StarFiSH

Ok, now time to add this starfish to the ocean bottom. Hey look, he already has a friend.

If you want your starfish to be a bead, use a needle tool to gently pierce between two arms. Ease in a piece of thicker wire to hold that hole open if you want. Remove the wire after baking.

# Know your Local Starfish

Ella is sneaking away from the incoming tide in this bead. (Did you notice the little wave canes?)

This is Sparky, who is hanging out here in this mini ocean scene, trying to look swelligent.

These triplets are known simply as "Them" in the seedy underworld of Groggy Reef. It's better if you don't know about them. In fact, forget I even brought it up.

Lord Sandybottom was named by Jeffey, who was on holiday with his family and found him in a tidepool. Ol' Bottom, as he is known to his friends, now resides in an old pickle jar with some shells, a hermit crab named Midge and a plastic palm tree. On Monday, he is going to go to Show and Tell. He is very excited about it, and has been practicing his wiggling, to better impress the children.

Meet Flopsy, Mopsy and Cottontail. Hmmm. They are a bit confused as to which book they are in, exactly.

Cosmos is not a starfish. He is a visitor from another planet many light centuries away and came to answer the question of life, the universe, and everything in it. He got distracted however by the pleasures of this planet - the caress of a gentle wind after a rain, the colors of a beautiful sunset, chocolate. Maybe he got his answer after all.

Mello is cool, man. That's all you need to know.

Oh yeah,
if you want to, you can add real shells to your ocean scene - sometimes a few here and there are a nice touch! I've found that if you use liquid clay to fill up the shell's hole and then press the shell opening into the clay, the liquid clay will bond to the regular clay and make a secure bond. You can add a dab of the liquid clay to the spot you're attaching it to, if you want to really seal the deal.

# Seahorse Roundup

Ya gotta have a seahorse for your ocean. Ya just gotta!

There are two ways to start your seahorse. Easiest is to make a ball of clay about the size of a boiled egg yolk. Roll and pinch to make a long teardrop shape. The other way is to make a lookat blend until you have something that amuses you. Roll it up tightly to preserve the coolest section of the blend, and remove any parts that bore you (it will probably be longer than you need, so you can nip off any extra). Now make that long teardrop shape.

For this color I used a mixture of white and pearl, and added a bit of ecru, turquoise, green pearl and blue pearl.

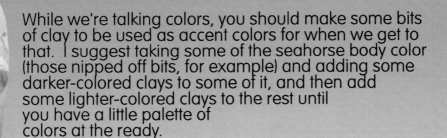

While we're talking colors, you should make some bits of clay to be used as accent colors for when we get to that. I suggest taking some of the seahorse body color (those nipped off bits, for example) and adding some darker-colored clays to some of it, and then add some lighter-colored clays to the rest until you have a little palette of colors at the ready.

Now take the teardrop shape and pinch to make a neck, separating his head from the body. You'll want to squeeze gently, moving around the clay to leave about a half inch of clay on top for the head. Don't make the neck too thin - unless you want a seagiraffe.

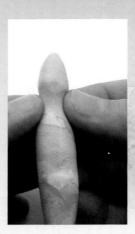

added a lot of blue pearl for this c

added a little blue pearl and ecru for this color

added white for this color

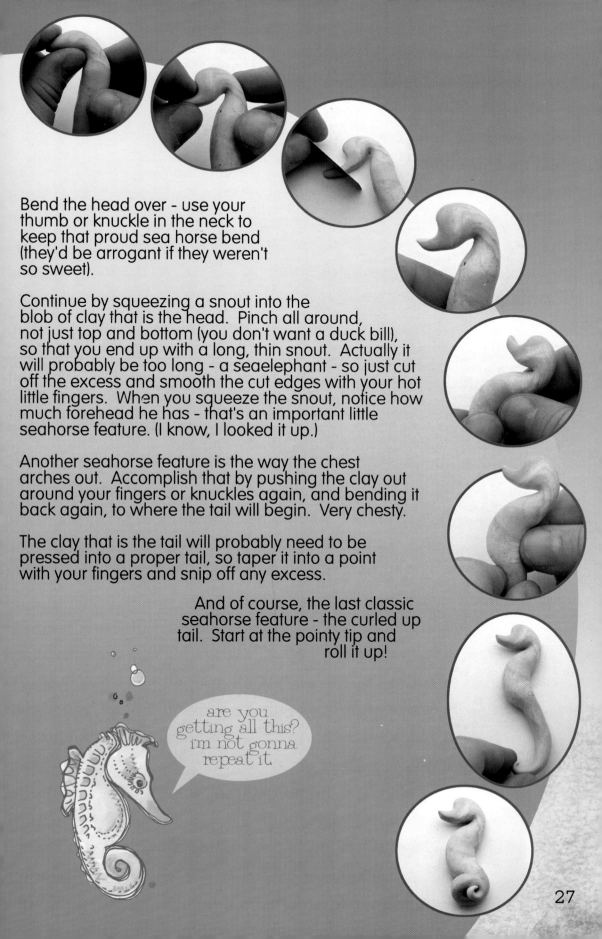

Bend the head over - use your thumb or knuckle in the neck to keep that proud sea horse bend (they'd be arrogant if they weren't so sweet).

Continue by squeezing a snout into the blob of clay that is the head. Pinch all around, not just top and bottom (you don't want a duck bill), so that you end up with a long, thin snout. Actually it will probably be too long - a seaelephant - so just cut off the excess and smooth the cut edges with your hot little fingers. When you squeeze the snout, notice how much forehead he has - that's an important little seahorse feature. (I know, I looked it up.)

Another seahorse feature is the way the chest arches out. Accomplish that by pushing the clay out around your fingers or knuckles again, and bending it back again, to where the tail will begin. Very chesty.

The clay that is the tail will probably need to be pressed into a proper tail, so taper it into a point with your fingers and snip off any excess.

And of course, the last classic seahorse feature - the curled up tail. Start at the pointy tip and roll it up!

are you getting all this? i'm not gonna repeat it

27

Eyes are really similar to the turtle, only you don't need to make the eye sockets - seahorse eyes bulge out. Make two contrasting clay balls, but don't pancake them, just press them gently onto either side of the head. Next, wire up two dark, round eye beads (same way as you did for the turtle eyes) and add them to each side of the head, in the center of that ball o' clay. Squash 'em in gently (there's a contradiction of terms, huh?) You can leave the eyes just like that, or you can add some little lines around his eyes (it's a seahorse thing) like rays around a sun. They can go all the way around, or just a little ways. Make them by gently pulling the ball of clay outward onto the clay of the head with a tool.

If you look at a picture of an actual real-live seahorse you'll notice the little waves of fins on the side of his body, back, neck and head sometimes, too. With this lil' guy, I've taken some liberties with reality and combined these into a stylized cluster of fin-ish-ness in the middle of the back and on the top of the head. I think it says "seahorse" without bogging down in anatomically correct detail, don't you? Plus it's just fun. So, let's make fin-ish-ness-es! (ok, now that really isn't a word!)

Start by selecting from your palette of accent clay colors and making little snakes of clay - rounded on one end and pointy on the other. Press them firmly into place in the middle of the back and into the body area a bit if you want to. Of course, the fins don't have to be snakes - they can be more round, or more square, or more some other shape. Just have fun. Vary the colors as you like. I like to add some of the same fins on top of the head like hair (I know seahorses don't have hair, but it looks good). These are rice shaped bits, and are laid down like shingles, starting with the most forward one and working back, one on top of the other. Press down on the part that touches the head to attach.

you can make him say 'oooh' with a little poke from a pointy tool

28

Continue adding clay accents, and those fun, fun beaded embellishments! Don't forget some dots of clay or other fun textures on his chest. It just looks good.

Finally the finishing touches. For more personality, give his head a little twist so he's turning to look at you a bit (no sense in spending all that extra effort to do both eyes if you're not going to see them, huh?)

Time to add Finster (I just think he looks like a "Finster," don't you?) to the ocean scene. Sea horses like to linger amongst the sea grasses, so let's tuck him in there. For a more firm connection with a minimum of smooshing, a gloop of liquid clay in the contact spot is a good idea. I've tucked a little pillow of tissue paper (the nose-blowing kind, not the wrapping presents kind) to hold his charming head tilt in place until he's done baking. (Yup, the tissue paper can go right into the oven.)

Alrighty then, our scene is looking mighty swell. Hmmmmm. Still needs something.

What's that? Oh, sure. (Finster just asked me if he could invite his buddy Slick to be a part of this scene. Slick is a fish.) You know I'm making this all up right? Polymer clay seahorses can't talk. (No vocal cords.)

## FocaL Bead

To make your seahorse into a focal bead, he'll need to have a hole for stringing. I usually make this before I start adding on too many embellishments or there'll be mushing. Gently twist a needle tool through the top of his chest, right below the neck (it's more sturdy there, but it will still hang well). Twist it back out and insert that thicker wire to hold the hole open throughout the sculpting. Remove the wire after it's finished baking and cooling. Hide the hole with clay dots on the chest, and the fins on the back -- no one will even see it!

29

# Some other seahorses, for various reasons.

For this seahorse, I used gold clay and large lapis beads. As you can tell, I just skipped the whole fin concept and went for an overall body decor of curlicues. He continues to break tradition by having his tail curl the other way.

These fins are the roundy version. Accent beads of amethyst and flourite are tucked in here and there.

Lots of pearl clay and freshwater pearl accent beads here. I skipped the arched chest, too, cuz he's trying o be inconspicuous.

Ok, lots of neck arch here, I don't know why - trying to see if there's any lint in his belly button, maybe. The coin pearls make an unusual accent feature, dontcha' think?

I had some lovely faceted labradorite stones, with a hole drilled on the bottom, allowing them to lay like gemstones. Because of the greyblue shine of the stones, I made the seahorse's clay to match. Little wired strings of glass beads make an interesting addition, as well as the little dots of clay with indentations in them -- he's fruit loopy!

This little guy is off to the races! You can tell because his tail is in "zoom" mode!

Thought you might like to see another option for tails -- the corkscrew version. If any strong ocean currents come by he'll be gripping on tight to the nearest kelp strand. The beads in the fin section are jade.

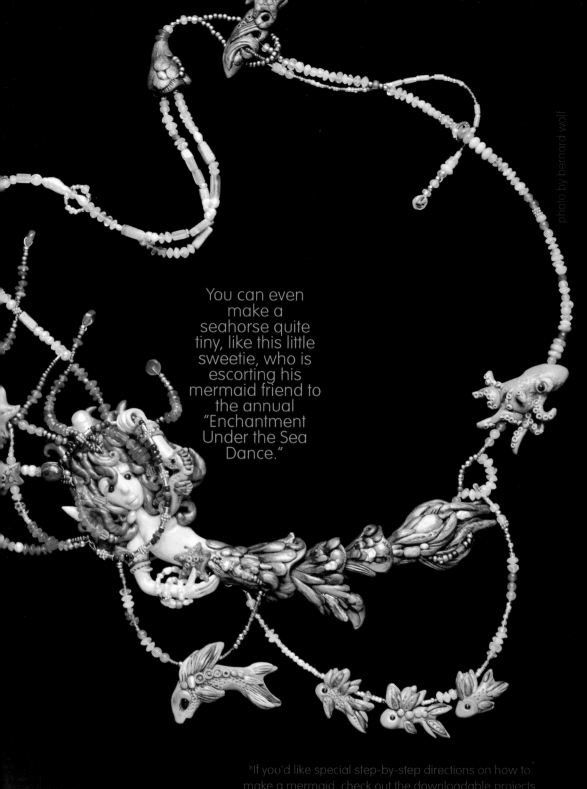

You can even
make a
seahorse quite
tiny, like this little
sweetie, who is
escorting his
mermaid friend to
the annual
"Enchantment
Under the Sea
Dance."

photo by bernard wolf

*If you'd like special step-by-step directions on how to
make a mermaid, check out the downloadable projects
at www.cforiginals.com

# Let's get FISHY with it

## colors

Anything goes - whatever color you're in the mood for. I'm going to make a yellowy fish because that will stand out nicely in the bluegreen scene. I used Premo's cadmium yellow, pearl and gold for the mix. (My personal preference is for more earthy tones in all my color mixes so I almost always add a little gold or a little ecru. Or a little both.) Make some lighter and darker versions, like we did for the seahorse, so you will have your palette for later accents. I added white to make a lighter mix and gold to make a darker version.

Start with a ball of clay (the main body color) about the same size as for the seahorse - maybe a little smaller. Roll it into a log and then squeeze as if you were making a neck for the seahorse again, only this time it will be to separate his body from his tail.

Flatten this shape slightly with your fingers.

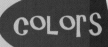

don't mind me, I'm just sitting here being cute

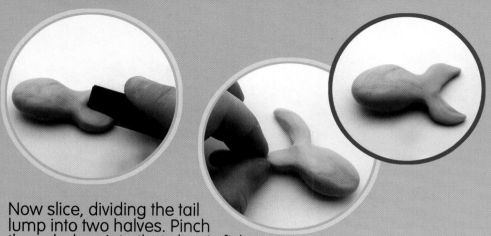

Now slice, dividing the tail
lump into two halves. Pinch
those halves into that classic fishy
tail shape -- at this point he'll look like one of the little fish crackers.
Now go to the store and buy some of those little fishy crackers and
take a break for snacks. Oh, and get some cheese and salami to go
with them, since you're up anyway. You can't create on an empty
stomach, you know.

Now let's add fins, starting with the top fins. First,
make some round balls of clay (you can use any of
the colors you've got - I usually use the same body
color for this step, since most of these fin bits will
be covered up. Save the accent colors for the top
layers of fins where they'll be more visible.)
Roll the balls into snakes and flatten slightly.

Attach a row of fins to the top of the fish -
on the back side. You can pick him up
and press them on, or line them up on
your work space and then lay the fish
shape on top and press them firmly
together.

If you're going to make a fish
into a focal bead, this is the time to add
the wire for holding that string hole open.
Just lay it directly on top of the fin lineup.
Now add another layer of fins. (If the wire is
there, cover it completely with the new fins. If
you're not adding a wire, make the second lineup anyway, it will add body and shine. No wait,
that's shampoo and conditioner that do that.
It will just add fin-y goodness.) Use the same
body color for these if you want to, we'll get
more fancy soon.

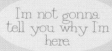
I'm not gonna
tell you why I'm
here.

Do the same to the tail flukes-- add snakes of clay to build up the look of fins.

He needs a bottom fin, too. Use your finger to press a groove into the belly area, towards the head. Now make a larger teardrop shape, flatten it and press it into the finger groove. I suggest also adding an identical fin shape behind it (press it onto the back of the fish, touching the front fin). It adds stability if you're making a bead, but it's a matter of personal taste to add it or not when you're making a fish for to an ocean scene, like we are now.

Ok, remember I said we'd get fancy with the fins. Well, here we go. When you mixed up some colors for the palette, did you do the lookat blend trick and get some interesting patterns?

Oh goodie - here's how to use those. Find a likely-looking section. Slice out a bit with your blade, now bend it and then gently press that bend into a snake (you can't just roll it or you'll lose the fun streaks!) See? Doesn't that make an interesting potential fin bit? Press it on, over the boring yellow ones. Nice. Now make a bunch more and press them on top of all the fin areas until you have a nicely balanced look.

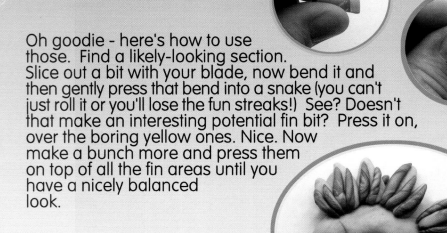

I pressed in a little suggestion of a gill with the knifey edge of my favorite wooden tool, just for fun.

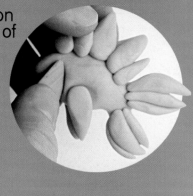

Eye time! Same process as you did for all the other eyeballed creatures so far. Choose a bead (this one is a 4mm garnet), wire it up, place a ball of contrasting-color clay in the appropriate eye zone, flatten like a pancake and squoosh in the eye bead, wire-side first. Press it in good for maximum cuteness. (You only have to do one eye for the fish, no one will see the back side).

Now, what does he need? A motorcycle? No, silly me. More fins? Yes! We haven't used that nice white-ish-yellowy color yet.

After you've added all the fins you want (or run out of room to cram anymore on, as in the case with this guy), you'll want to consider your beaded embellishment options. You can go for the individually-wired beads-here-and-there-look, or a line-of-jewels-down-the-center-of-the-body look. I went with the second one. These are faceted citrine beads.

Lastly, if you want to use all the tricks in the bag, add some texture. (These are just dimples pressed in with a dowel.) They will really stand out when it comes time to add the patina.

Ok, Slick Fish is looking pretty slick indeed, and time to add him to the ocean scene. Use a gloop of liquid clay and press firmly but carefully. If you're feeling energetic, or have had too much coffee, make a whole school of fish! Ok, maybe that's overdoing it a bit, but here's a whole school of fish to look at anyway (and give you ideas for the next fish you do.)

The pattern on this nosey little guy was made by rolling the grip of a needle tool over the surface.

This is a big bead of kyanite which has a lot of shine to it. He's grinning about that, sorta'. Notice the curls that hide the ends of the wire from the large bead.

Well, the hairdo just got out of control here. Still, once you start making dots, you just can't stop.

This fish is late for the Enchantment Under the Sea Dance. Maybe that hot mermaid will dance with him.

As you can tell by now, these fish are stylized realism, not actually realistic. This allows for more flights of artistic fancy, like this bouffant fin explosion.

This guy hopes he'll get to The Dance before that other guy.

Here's another really cool tool, it's a scaler, used in taxidermy. As you probably expected, it makes really wonderful scales - see! (if you want to know where to find one, check the back of the book.)

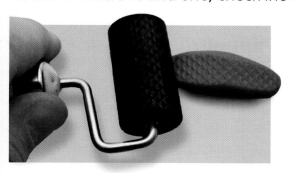

Sometimes a well-placed single bead here and there can accent just right.

These curls are certainly not found in nature, but they look cool, huh? The lineup of moonstone in the center of the body adds sparkle.

Sweet and simple.

This fish is adorned with opal chips that had an especially nice glow to them. For some reason the patina-ing process really brings out the fire in opals.

This guy has a mouth, something I don't do often, but probably should. Mabé pearls are tucked into the fins and really add an interesting contrast.

These are loosely coiled snail curls, and a cluster of citrine.

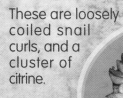

This one has always been one of my favorites. I don't know why.

Well, it is done, but of course now we will need a way to hang it.

There are a couple of hanging options. At this stage, we can bake the whole piece for 20 minutes, let it cool, and then add a wire loop (or two) to the back side for it to hang from. Or we can add some wire-reinforced loops of clay to the top, and hang it up directly through those, or we can pierce some holes in the top to allow a cord, ribbon, or beaded cable to loop through. Or you can just pay someone to stand next to the wall and just hold it up forever.

Here's how to do each of those options - you pick which one you want!

# Hanger in the back

First, bake your piece for a short time, just to set it. 275°F for about 20 minutes or so is usually plenty. Let it cool. Remember that it is very fragile at this point. It has begun to harden, but it isn't hard yet, so pointy bits will be quite breakable.

Make one or two wire hangers. I like to use copper wire that is at least 18 gauge (16 or 14 is even better for a larger piece like this ocean scene). Curve it with pliers into a U-shape. Then bend at least one end outward - anything from a slight angle to a full U is fine - what you want to do is make sure the wire will not ever pull out from the finished piece (you know gravity, it's always trying stuff like that).

Now, gloop on some liquid clay and lay the wire hanger on top of that (loop side up of course). Sandwich it with a top piece of flattened clay (pancake shape again). Press the clay around the wire firmly, anchoring it in. You can make one hanger in the center or two or more, spaced along the back. The bigger the piece, the more hangers you may want.

One word of caution - press the clay on by cushioning the piece in your hands so that you absorb the pressing - you don't want to lay it face-down on a hard surface and start pushing because things will go snap! If an accident does happen, just finish up the back, then give it another quick cook to set the hangers (15 or 20 minutes is fine) and then go back and repair any oopsies with liquid clay and fresh polymer clay. The liquid clay allows fresh clay to be added to baked clay. It does need to be baked just the same as if it were regular polymer clay, once you're done.

*All the details for baking and patina-ing are at the end of the book (which is almost here), so check that section out for all the details!

The nifty thing about polymer clay is that you can do these little bakes as often as you want without hurting anything. Once you're ready for the final, finishing bake, though -- act as though you haven't baked it at all and go for the full time (check that baking section in the back for details.)

# Wire-reinForced clay LoopS:

Start with a thick snake of clay (a good idea is to use whatever clay color is in the section that you are going to be adding this to) and curl it into a loop. Flatten slightly and attach it to the back of the scene towards one corner. (You don't need to pre-bake anything for this procedure.) Now cut and curve a piece of wire to match the loop - it will go right on top of the clay. Make sure the loop will reach all the way onto the main background clay, for stability.)

Make a second snake of clay and curl it to match the one on the back side, and press it right on top, sandwiching the wire inside.

Repeat on the opposite corner of your scene to match, and it's ready to bake.

# Pierce HoLeS:

This is the simplest. With a dowel tool or similar, pierce a hole into the top corner and "stir" it to widen the hole. Do the same on the opposite corner. Pick a spot that looks nicest in the design and make the hole wide enough to accommodate a beading cable or some other hanging cord. Usually, I make the hole large enough so that I can put beads on the cable that goes through the hole - so that no raw cable is exposed. Looks nicer, I think.

I don't even need a hanger 'cuz I'm a sculpture.

# Octopus

Well, what do you say to one last sea creature? Yeah. I thought so - octopus it is. You know they are highly intelligent, very mysterious creatures. And of course, fun to make in clay because they have those wavy tentacles with all the suckers.

Start with a clay mix, as always -- this one is ecru and gold and a little green and some white - you know, octopus color.

Make a ball of clay, and then form it into a button mushroom shape - an oval with a knob on the end. The knob will be the head, the rest will be sliced to make the eight legs. First, cut it in half (up to the knob) and then each half into half and half again -- if you do it right, you'll end up with eight slices that are all roughly the same thickness.

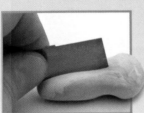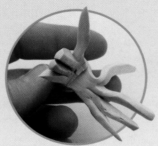

Keep them spread open so they don't stick together, and press and pinch and smooth until all the tentacles look octopus-ish.

Form the knob into a head by pinching and bending - it should be like a paper sack full of oatmeal - droopy, but solid.

I suggest making a bit of a background piece for him to sit on (as a pendant or wall piece, or you can cover a glass jar with oceany color clay and press him onto that!) This way, you can get all swiggley with the tentacles without having to worry         about them breaking off.

Press the octopus, as he is so far, onto the background clay and then arrange the tentacles - go for graceful curls and swirls!

Add an eye the same way as we did for the seahorse -- ball of clay with a wired dark bead pressed into the center.

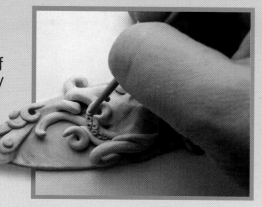

Now add suckers - lots and lots of suckers! Use little tiny balls of clay (I used a slightly darker color clay) and press them into the tentacles with the tip of a pointy-ish tool (this is a knitting needle). Follow the underneath side of each tentacle as it twists and curls.

Last, add any other beads as accents and make holes for stringing it.

Now it's ready to bake.

This is for when you want to bridge the gap between elegant and weird. This is a spectacular piece of art glass. Just the thing a many-tentacled beastie from the deep would wear to the Enchantment Under the Sea Dance. With any luck he'll catch the eye of the belle of the ball, that swell gal, the Mermaid.

The copper loop goes all the way through the bead and anchors into the clay head. There is another, smaller loop of copper tucked among the tentacles so this bead can be hung from both and make a real conversation piece as the focal point of a necklace.

It's not any real sea creature - sort of a nautilus/cuttlefish/ squid thingy. It's always nice to make imaginary creatures that look believable - it keeps people guessing!

Here's a little extra project that's quick and easy and oceany --

## a FiSHy bookmark!

Start by making an oceany blend of clay and running it through a thinner setting of the pasta machine (about halfway on the dial). Cut out a freeform wavey shape.

Use a marker to trace a design onto a piece of tracing paper. (for some designs, go to my website for free downloads!)

Press the pattern gently into the clay by tracing it with a pointy dowel tool, or something similar.

Now cook it at 275°F for 10-15 minutes. Let it cool.

With a permanent marker (I used a Sharpie brand pen) trace the indents.

Pour a gloop of liquid clay onto the bookmark and spread it over the surface evenly.

Decorate it with markers, embossing powders, PearlEx powders, glitters, tiny glass hole-less beads or any other oven-friendly embellishment.

Bake again for 20-30 minutes at 275°F. Cool. Add some funky fringe and knot in some beads. Now go read a book!

## official glossary
of CF words, as used in this book,
in no particular order

smoosh - to squoosh down a little bit.

squoosh - to smoosh down a little bit.

wad - a bit. Less than a clump and more than a smidgen.

cane/caner - polymer clay is an ideal medium for making canes. No, not the kind you use for a little extra support when the ol' legs are hurting, but the kind of pieced-together patterns of clay, manipulated into long rods, or canes, and then sliced into thin slivers and used in all kinds of interesting ways. A caner is someone who makes canes (obviously).

cheatin' canes - same concept as canes in that it is a pattern made up of layers of clay and used by slicing off slivers and applying them to interesting projects. They are "cheating" because the piecing together is quick and loose, not precise and controlled. Usually you only get a little of the pattern. But hey, if you want a lot, then you just have to take the time, effort, patience, control and self-discipline of real caning. Nah.

splooch - a blob, as in "Darn, I stepped in a splooch of ketchup."

lookat blend - what you get when you mix clays together with the intent of producing streaks, smears and swells of color. Named for the exclamation you shout when it works, as in "Hey! Lookat this cool color blend I just made!"

dab - just a little bit, like a smidgen

smidgen - just a little bit, like a dab

gloop - a squeeze of liquid clay. It helps to actually say "Gloop!" as you squeeze the liquid clay out of the bottle. Ok, it doesn't help at all, it's just fun to say.

snippet - just a little bit, like say half an inch. Usually a snippet of wire. I don't know why.

fin-ish-ness - the appearance of fins, without being anatomically correct. plural: fin-ish-ness-es

chocolate - a necessary feature of creativity. Spend the money if you can for the good stuff.

ramblings - a meandering of speech or writing. I do this a lot, like the time I was teaching a class, and told the story of how my mom once made beer jello for dinner, when I was a child. Yup, jello made from beer for some reason with bits of chicken and carrots in it. No it didn't taste good. It was jello made from beer, with chicken in it. This story explains a lot about me actually. See, rambling - like that.

swiggley - in a manner that is swigglish; pertaining to or referring to swiggling; acting in a manner to cause swigglement.

smears, stretch marks, crinkles and swooshes - some things you want to have in a lookat blend, as opposed to some things we have, but don't want, as we get older.

43

As promised, here's the why and how for adding a patina to your finished pieces. After the clay has baked and completely cooled, you can add a patina if you want to. This is an optional step and if you've never done it before, it's a good idea to practice on a piece that you don't care about, to get the hang of it before tackling your masterpiece! Adding a patina is the same as antiquing -- brushing color onto the piece, then wiping it off the surfaces to leave it only in the cracks and details. It can add richness and depth.

I use acrylic paint (Basics by Liquitex is my brand of choice, although any acrylic paint will do) and I usually patina in various shades of browns. Obviously other colors will work too.

Your paintbrush should be just damp and the paint should be the consistency of mayonnaise. Brush it over the surface, really forcing the paint into the cracks and textures. Work only a small amount at a time, an inch or two at the most -- acrylic paint dries quickly.

With a well-rung out sponge, wipe the paint off the surface. Use multiple sponges to wipe so that the piece stays clean and not "muddy" from too much paint smeared around.

Keep working until the piece is done to your liking. Remember you don't have to patina the entire piece - sometimes just here and there is great. I also like to patina the ocean in blue instead of brown sometimes to keep the "polluted" look from happening - or just don't patina it at all.

Let it dry thoroughly. Now it's done, or you can add a clear coating to protect the patina, giving it that professional, finished look.

I coat my pieces with Flecto brand Veriahane (a waterbased outdoor varnish.) I like the low shine and it really seems to work well with polymer. I also use Sculpey's Satin Glaze sometimes. There are other products available too.

Don't varnish over the beads! The finish will actually dull the stones and pearls as it will leave a plasticky layer on them.

When all is done and dry, place it on a clean piece of cardstock and pop it back in the oven for a last bake for 15-20 minutes at 200°F.

Ta-da!

Lookat blends are a wonderful way to make neat color patterns happen. Start with your clays, and clump them together so that they are all on the top, right where you can keep your eyes on them, and run it through the pasta machine.

Look this over and fold it (like a pleat, only sloppy) so that the best color possibilities stay on the top. Run it through again and keep repeating the process - look for the best blend possibilities and fold, rip and gather to keep them in the visible area. Don't let the good stuff get folded into the center and lost. Change the direction that you feed the clay into the machine often - it can bring unexpected and interesting results. Lookat! an oceany blend!

**A word about copying, copyright infringement, and how to use what you've learned in this book.**

Once you've read this book (and the other books in the CF series) and started making the fun projects, and showing them off to friends and family, then what? Where does my art stop and yours begin? What's legal, ethical, polite?

Here's what I expect. I want you to have fun making the projects and sharing them. I hope that you will experiment and grow in creativity and use the ideas to follow your own artistic journey. If I didn't expect you to make these projects, then I shouldn't have put them in a book. However, when you cross over to selling your work, I would expect that you would add some of your own individuality to the pieces and make changes. The copyright laws do require three substantial changes to a piece to avoid infringing on another artist's work. So, if you do want to sell pieces that look a lot like my work, please make sure you make a sign, or add text to a website and plainly state next to your work that it is "inspired by the work of Christi Friesen" (you could add a "www.CForiginals.com too, so others could find my books -- I wouldn't mind!) -- this way we all win. You get to learn, have fun, and even sell, and I get acknowledgment as the originator of the design, and maybe some book sales.

You will have to use your own judgment to determine if your work is close enough to need the "inspired by", or enough of your own touch to stand on its' own! If you want to teach my designs to others, contact me, it's a bit trickier! (www.cforiginals.com and click the contact button.) Happy claying!

# Polymer Clay: An Overview

Polymer clay is a wonderful medium. It is colorful, durable, easy to use. Condition the polymer clay by warming up smaller amounts in your hands and kneading, stretching or rolling the clay. A pasta machine is of course the most useful tool ever invented for polymer clay (and you thought it was for making spaghetti.) Conditioning the clay is crucial to the final durability of the piece. As the clay ages, its component ingredients regroup, so to speak, and need to be redistributed to their "original" state. Unconditioned clays are more susceptible to cracking during baking.

Many brands of polymer clay are available, all are essentially composed of the same basic ingredients. Each brand has its own recommended uses, such as caning, sculpting, doll-making, etc. For most sculpture projects, any brand of polymer clay can be used or mixed with other brands yielding satisfactory results. I use and recommend Premo! brand, made by Sculpey, as a clay especially suited for sculpture use.

Many tools can be used when working with polymer clay -- wood, metal and plastic are equally functional. Tools manufactured for traditional clay and ceramic modeling, such as those by Kemper Tools, are an ideal choice. Since polymer clay does not thin down with water, you will rely on your tools and your fingers to manipulate, smooth and texture the clay. All tools used for polymer clay should not be used for food afterwards.

You can choose to work on any flat, nonporous work surface, such as glass, or marble, but wood can absorb the plasticizers in the clay, staining the wood and hardening your clay. I recommend sculpting on a piece of thick paper card stock. You should not store your clay on card stock, as it will absorb plasticizers from the clay also. You can store your clay on wax paper or in plastic sandwich bags or other nonporous containers.

Cleaning your hands when switching colors so as not to transfer residual color from hands to clay is important. So is cleanup when you are finished claying. Boraxo or some other gritty cleanser is very helpful in removing the residue. You can also use baby wipes, cold cream, baby oil or rubbing alcohol before soap and water washing.

Baking polymer clay is best accomplished with a home oven or convection oven, although toaster ovens can be adequate when the temperature is supervised, as they have a tendency to overheat (I suspect gremlins). Temperature is critical in the curing of polymer clay. Clay that is cooked at too low a temperature or for too short a time will not adequately cure and can be brittle and easily broken. Always use an oven thermometer and follow the clay manufacturers instructions. Do not cook at too high a temperature, or clay will burn. Always use adequate ventilation. Do not microwave. Bake in a pan or on a ceramic tile that is designated for clay use only (keep the finished piece on the cardstock before placing it in your cooking pan/tile to prevent the surface touching metal or tile from becoming shiny). If you use a home oven, you should clean the oven before using it for food baking.

On average, baking time for sculpture is a minimum of 20 minutes for every quarter inch of thickness at the thickest part of the clay. For most pieces this means a minimum of 30-45 minutes in the oven. I usually bake my pieces for at least an hour or more.

Cured clay is very durable - so you can pass on your masterpieces as heirlooms to your children and to their children, and their children, and eBay.

If you can't finish your project all in one go and want to store it until you can get back to it, take it off the cardstock and place it in a ziploc bag and seal it -- this will keep the dust off until you're ready to play.

# Resources

## clay, tools & equipment

Of course there are lots of places to get everything you need for the projects in this book . . . and beyond! Bead and craft stores carry most things, and you can order online with the click of a mouse. Here's a few of my favorites:

www.ClayFactory.net -- tell 'em Christi sent ya! This is the place I buy my favorite tools too (the interchangeable ones and the wooden AJ17). And of course they carry Premo! in all the colors and stamps and powders and on and on.

For more info on Premo! clay and other Sculpey products, visit: www.Sculpey.com

For that taxidermy scaling tool, check www.vandykestaxidermy.com (part #01001346)

www.FireMountainGems.com is a great place for beads, findings and tools!

And of course, the most fun way to buy beads, pearls and art glass is always to see them, feel them, and justify buying more than you need at a bead show! For starters look into the To Bead True Blue show held yearly at the end of January in Tucson, AZ. at the Manning House during the big Tucson show week (www.tobeadtrueblue.com), and the annual Bead & Button show (www.BeadandButtonshow.com) held in Milwaukee, WI in the summer.

## information

www.NPCG.org is the National Polymer Clay Guild website. Check it out for polymer guilds, events and classes.

www.PolymerClayCentral.com will connect you to every juicy tidbit of information, opinion, and news in the wide, wide world of polymer clay. If it's happening in polymer clay, it'll wander through here.

http://groups.yahoo.com/group/cforiginals is my chat group where the nicest group of polymer enthusiasts swap stories, accomplishments and encouragement. Join us!

www.PolkaDotCreations.com is a wonderful source for books, articles and magazines that have to do with polymer clay.

PolymerCafe magazine is devoted entirely to polymer clay happenings, projects, people. Many other magazines regularly feature polymer articles and projects, too.

## art glass beads

There are so many wonderful glass artists to discover. Here are the ones whose beads are in this book:

John Winter --
www.winterglas.com

Robin Foster --
www.FosterFireGlass.com

Jennifer Ringer --
www.SirensSongDesigns.net

Cheryl Harris --
chelyha55@yahoo.com

Doug Remschneider--
www.Remschneiderglass.com

47

"Dragons" is the first book in the CF Beyond Projects Sculpture series. It leads you through the process of creating dragons from polymer clay with humorous dialog, creative suggestions, interesting asides, lavish pictures, and even several dragon " personality profiles". This is more than just a project book, it's a fun read!

Detailed photos, step-by step instructions and a quirky sense of humor make this 2nd book in the series a great way to explore sculpting with polymer clay, no matter what your skill level. You will enjoy making exotic leaves, flowers, furry creatures, bugs and frogs, and adding embellishments to your creations, using pearls, semi-precious stones and beads.

Next in the series

This book is just full of feline fun. The big cats - lions and tigers and pumas, (oh my!) will roar to life as focal beads, masks and sculptures. But not to be outdone, a parade of kitties will show who really rules. Throughout the book, embellishments of beads, fibers and surface treatments will make this a book you want to cuddle up with.